Beginners Guide to Crochet

by Kirsty Pedlingham

Index

The Key Techniques

Crochet Patterns

UK/US Converstion Chart

Notes

The Key Techniques

Getting Started

This book is about learning the basic stitches.
Your ideal tools are a 5mm hook and some DK yarn
as these are used in all the crochet patterns.
However you can use whatever size hook and yarn
you have to hand, a larger sizes would be eaiser.

Just a quick note
I am using UK terms but there is a handy
UK/US conversion chart at the end of this booklet.

Are you ready to learn the basic stitches?

First you need a Slipknot

You firstly need to make a slipknot, the beginnings of all crochet makes. Find the end of your yarn and make a small loop. Pull a new loop from the yarn leading to the ball through the first loop. Gently tighten onto the hook and this is your first stitch.

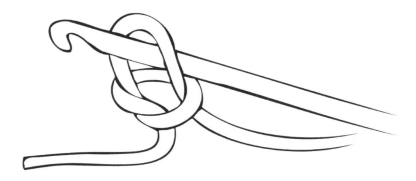

Next how to hold it

Now the yarn is on your hook, how do hold your hook and yarn. The picture below show you technically the correct way. If you have never crochet before then this might not feel right or be uncomfortable. There is no right or wrong, I just want you to be comfortable and you need to decide which way is best for you.

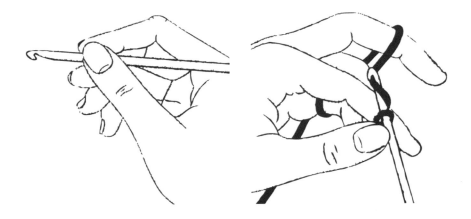

Now you are all set to learn the basic stitches.

Chain stitch - ch

Many crochet items start with a length of chain stitches and it often appears in patterns.

Firstly, when you wrap the yarn around the hook you will from the back over the hook, then down and under the hook. This is the same with all the basic stitches. Pull the hooked yarn through the current loop to create a new stitch. The chain stitch is completed.

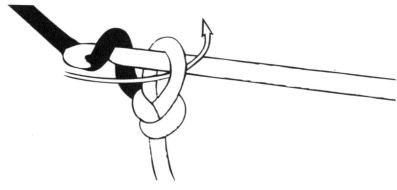

Slip stitch - ss

A stitch that joins stitches or allows you to move to a new place. Place you hook through the required stitch of you work and then wrap the yarn around the hook. Pull the yarn through both stitches on your hook to complete the stitch.

Double crochet - dc

This is one of the most commonly used stitches. Insert the hook at the required stitch. Wrap the yarn around the hook and pull it through the stitch. You now have two loops on the hook [Fig 1]. Now take the yarn around the hook again and pull it through both stitches to finish the stitch [Fig 2].

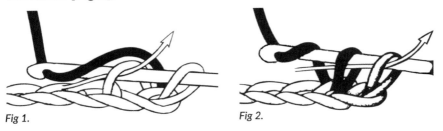

Fig 1.   Fig 2.

Treble - tr

This stitch is taller than a double crochet and adds height to you work. Firstly, wrap the yarn around the hook before you insert the hook into the required stitch [Fig 3]. Wrap the yarn around the hook again and pull the yarn through the stitch. You should now have 3 loops on the hook [Fig 4]. Wrap the yarn over the hook and pull it through 2 loops, leaving 2 loops left on the hook. Wrap the yarn around a last time and pull it though both of loops to complete the stitch [Fig 5].

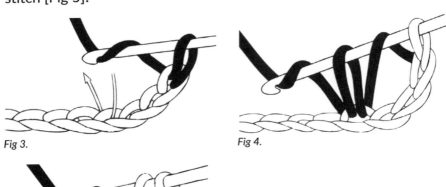

Fig 3.   Fig 4.

Fig 5.

Half treble - htr

This is a half way stitch between the double crochet and treble stitch. You start the same as the treble and get to 3 loops on the hook. Wrap the yarn around the hook and pull it through all 3 loops to complete the stitch.

Double treble - dtr

This stitch is a larger variation of the treble stitch. Here you need to wrap the yarn around the hook twice before you insert it into the required stitch [Fig 6]. Wrap the yarn around the hook and pull it through the stitch. You now have 4 loops on the hook [Fig 7].

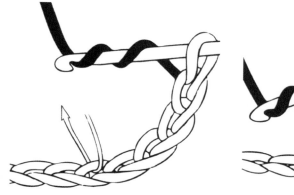

Fig 6.

Fig 7.

Wrap the yarn around again and pull it through the first 2 loops and you have 3 loop left on hook [Fig 8]. Wrap the yarn around again and pull it through the first 2 loops. Finally wrap the yarn around again and pull it through remaining 2 loops to complete the stitch [Fig 9].

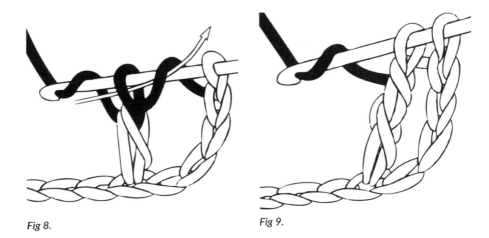

Fig 8.

Fig 9.

Taller treble variations

Triple Treble - ttr/Quad Treble - qtr

These are variations of the double treble only you wrap the yarn 3 or 4 time before inserting into the required stitch.

Magic Ring - mr

You are likely to use this stitch at the start of hats, gloves or toys. It allows you pull tight and make a closed circle. A set of chain stitches can be made into a circle with a slip stitch, but it will have a small space in the centre.

To start make a simple loop and insert the hook through it. Wrap the yarn around the hook and pull it through to form a loop [Fig 10]. Wrap the yarn around the hook and pull it through the loop on the hook [Fig 11].

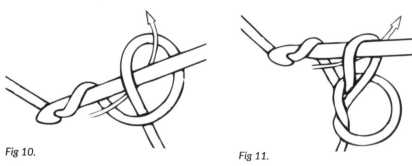

Fig 10.

Fig 11.

Wrap the yarn around again and pull it through to complete the first stitch on your ring [Fig 12]. Now insert your hook into the original ring and double crochet around until you have the required stitches [Fig 13].

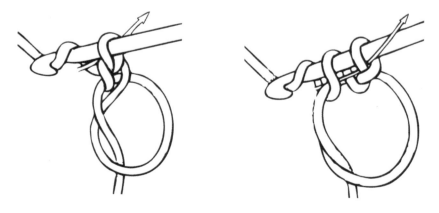

Fig 12.

Fig 13.

You can then pull down and tighten the ring. Finally slip stitch into the first stitch to make closed ring [Fig 14].

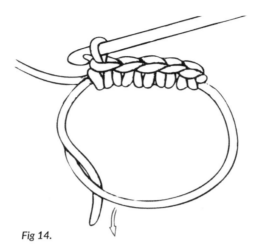

Fig 14.

Congratulations

You have mastered some of the basic stitches.
Now it is time to try a simple pattern.

Crochet Patterns

Cup Cosy

Materials & Tools:
- 100g DK yarn
- 5mm hook
- wool needle
- scissors

Cosy
Ch 31
Row 1: htr in 2nd from hook and every st to end, sl st to 1st htr to make a ring, ch. 30sts.
Rnd 2 - 9: htr in each st, sl st into first st of round, ch. 30sts. Fasten off.

Flower
5dc in mr.
Rnd 1: 2dc in every st, change colour. 10sts.
Rnd 2: ((dc, htr, tr, 2dtr) in first st, (2dtr, tr, htr, dc) in 2nd st) repeat in next 2sts to make more petals. Fasten off.

Finishing:
Sew in loose ends. Sew flower to the middle of the cosy.

Mug Cosy

Materials & Tools:
- 100g DK yarn
- 5mm hook
- button
- wool needle
- scissors

Ch 36
Row 1: htr in 2nd from hook and every st to end, turn, ch. 35sts.
Row 2: htr in every st to end, turn, ch. 35sts.
Row 3: htr in every st to end, ch11, turn. 45sts.
Row 4: htr in 2nd from hook and every st to end, ch, turn. 45sts.
Row 5: htr in next 41sts, ch2, miss 2sts, htr in last 2sts, turn, ch. 45sts.
Row 6: htr in every st to end. ch, turn. 45sts.
Row 7: htr in next 35sts, turn, ch. 35sts.
Row 8 – 9: htr in every st to end, turn, ch. 35sts. Fasten off.

Finishing:
Attach button roughly 4sts from the edge in the middle. Sew in any loose ends.

Granny Square

Materials & Tools:
- 100g DK yarn
- 5mm hook
- button
- wool needle
- scissors

Ch4 and sl st together to form a ring.

Rnd 1: ch3 (is 1st tr), 2tr, ch2, (3tr, ch2) three times into ring, sl st to join to the 3rd ch st of 1st tr, 2sl st over top of tr cluster and 1sl st into ch sp.

Rnd 2: ch3 (is 1st tr) 2tr, ch2, 3tr, ch2 into 1st ch sp, (3tr, ch2) twice into each ch sp, sl st to join to the 3rd ch st of 1st tr, 2sl st over top of tr cluster and 1sl st into ch sp.

Rnd 3: ch3 (is 1st tr) 2tr, ch2, 3tr, ch2 into 1st ch sp, *(3tr, ch2) once into middle ch sp and twice into corner ch sp* repeat* three times, sl st to join to the 3rd ch st of 1st tr, 2sl st over top of tr cluster and 1sl st into ch sp.

Finishing:
Cast off and sew loose ends.

You can continue to add as many rounds as you desire. Always start with ch3 as your 1st tr plus 2tr to make your 1st 3tr cluster.

Separate each 3tr cluster with 2ch. Ensure you have two 3tr clusters in each corner and one 3tr cluster in each of the spaces along the edges.

You can cast off after each round and start a new colour to create a lovely pattern. Alternatively, if you are feeling confident, you could also change the colour of each round by bringing the new colour in with the last sl st into the ch sp, allowing you to start your 3ch of the next row in the new colour.

Flower Bookmark

Materials & Tools:
- Colour A - a green for leaf or stem 100g DK yarn
- Colour B - centre of flower 100g DK yarn
- Colour C - flower colour 100g DK yarn
- 5mm hook
- wool needle

Leaf and Stem
Make in colour A ch8.
Rnd 1 of leaf: 4tr in 4th ch from hook, tr in next ch, htr in next ch, dc in next ch, sl st, ch, sl st in final ch, turn to go down the other side of original ch, dc in next st, htr in next st, tr in next st, 4tr in last st and sl st to top of first tr.
Stem from base of leaf: to create the stem ch 35 (this will fit an A5 notebook) or as long as you want it to be, turn and dc every st back to leaf, sl st into first tr, cast off.

Flower
Make in colour B mr5
Rnd 1: 2dc in each st. 10sts.
Rnd 2: change to colour C (dc, 2tr in first st, 2tr, dc in next st this make a petal) repeat four more times, sl st in first st, cast off.

Finishing:
Sew flower to top of stem with leaf at other end.

Wash Cloth

Materials & Tools:
- 100g DK yarn
- 5mm hook
- wool needle
- scissors

Ch 33
Row 1: miss 2sts (counts a dc,) work tr in next st, (miss 2sts, dc, tr in next st) repeat to last 3sts, miss 2sts, dc in last st. 31sts
Row 2: ch (counts as dc), turn tr in first dc, (miss tr, dc, tr in next dc), repeat to end, dc in turning ch. 31sts
Repeat row 2 until cloth measures same as width, fasten off.

Finishing:
Sew in loose ends.

Headband

Materials & Tools:
- 100g DK yarn
- 5mm hook
- wool needle
- scissors

Ch 16
Row 1: htr in 2nd from hook, turn ch. 1st.
Row 2: 2htr in st, turn ch. 2 sts.
Row 3: 2htr in each st, turn ch. 4sts.
Row 4: 2htr in each st, turn ch 8sts.
Row 5: skip odd sts dc, tr in next even sts, turn ch. 8sts.
Row 6 - 64: repeat row 5. 8sts.
Row 65: htr in each st, turn ch. 8sts.
Row 66: 4htr2tog, turn ch. 4sts.
Row 67: 2htr2tog, turn ch. 2sts.
Row 68: 1htr2tog, ch16. Cast off.

Finishing:
Sew in loose ends.

UK/US Converson Terms

UK	US
Double crochet - dc	Single crochet - sc
Treble - tr	Double crochet - dc
Half treble - htr	Haft double crochet - hdc
Double treble - dtr	Treble - tr
Triple treble - ttr	Double treble - dtr
Double crochet 2 together - dc2tog	Single crochet 2 together - sc2tog
Half treble 2 together - htr2tog	Half double 2 together - hdc2tog

Notes

Printed in Great Britain
by Amazon